30 Days with
SAINT THÉRÈSE

30 Days with
SAINT THÉRÈSE

by

Thomas J. Craughwell

TAN Books
An Imprint of Saint Benedict Press, LLC
Charlotte, North Carolina

All quotes from *Story of a Soul* taken from the TAN Books edition, translated by Michael Day. Copyright 2010 by TAN Books, an Imprint of Saint Benedict Press, LLC.

ISBN: 978-1-935302-67-4

Cover design by Caroline Kiser.

Printed and bound in the United States of America.

TAN Books
An Imprint of Saint Benedict Press, LLC
Charlotte, North Carolina
2012 .

Biography of St. Thérèse

Devotion to St. Thérèse of Lisieux—popularly known as the Little Flower—is one of the religious phenomenon of the 20th century. Here was a young woman, scarcely known outside her circle of family and relatives, who died at age twenty-four in a Carmelite cloister, in an obscure French town; yet within a year or two of her death, her fame had spread around the Catholic world. Appeals for canonization were so insistent that the Holy See waived the traditional fifty-year waiting period. As a result, Thérèse was canonized in 1925, twenty-eight years after her death—which, given the exacting rules required for beatification and canonization at the time, was considered a record.

It was Thérèse's spiritual autobiography, *The Story of a Soul*, that brought her into the spotlight. At the heart of this brief memoir was a method

Thérèse called "the Little Way:" instead of striving for holiness through great acts of charity or penance, or even hoping for the grace of martyrdom, Thérèse urged her readers to perform every task during the day and bear every petty annoyance for no other purpose than the love of God. This was something anyone could do: mothers offered up the drudgery of cooking and cleaning; workers offered up the strain of their jobs; students the stress of their studies; children the scrapes and bruises they got while playing.

The Lisieux Carmel, where Thérèse had lived and died, released the first edition of *The Story of a Soul* on the first anniversary of her death—September 30, 1898. By 1910, it had sold 47,000 copies. By 1915, sales had soared to 150,000 copies. The simplicity and sweetness of Thérèse's book found a wide audience, but scholars of the great Catholic mystics observed that beneath the sentimental style of the book, Thérèse's ideas were rooted in the writings of St. John of the Cross, St. Teresa of Avila, and Thomas á Kempis' *Imitation of Christ*.

Of course, it takes more than a popular book to make a saint; to be frank, it takes a miracle. In fact, in the early 20th century the Church required four miracles—two for beatification, two for canonization. As Thérèse's cause for sainthood advanced, literally thousands of people across the globe attributed miracles to her intercession. At one point, the nuns at the Lisieux Carmel were receiving 500 letters a day, most of them describing inexplicable events which the correspondents attributed to the prayers of Thérèse.

Thérèse's biographers have observed that it is not entirely unexpected that she would find a religious vocation: there was a touch of the cloister to her childhood home. Her parents, Louis Martin and Azelie-Marie Guerin, had both tried to enter religious orders, but both had been turned away. Louis and Zelie were intensely pious, so much so that on their wedding night, Louis suggested they forego a regular married life to live as chastely as the Blessed Virgin and St. Joseph. At first, Zelie agreed. They lived chastely for 10 months until the advice of their spiritual director, combined with their desire to raise souls for heaven, changed their minds. Ultimately, the Martins would have nine children, five of whom survived to adulthood: Marie, Pauline, Leonie, Celine, and Thérèse.

Both Louis and Zelie operated their own businesses, and both did very well: she made Alençon lace, he was a watchmaker. In 1871, Louis received an offer for his business, which he accepted. The money he got from the sale combined with an inheritance and Zelie's earnings, enabled him to retire. Sadly, in 1878, Zelie died of breast cancer. His five daughters became Louis' chief comfort, Thérèse especially. He called her his "little queen," and he spoiled and pampered her, as did Thérèse's older sisters.

As the older girls matured, one by one they announced their intention of entering the religious life. Pauline joined the Lisieux Carmel, and soon Marie joined her there. Leonie entered a convent of Poor Clares, but she found that she was unsuited to such an austere life; after two months, the superior of the Poor Clares sent Leonie home.

On the afternoon of Pentecost Sunday, 1887, Thérèse approached her father as he sat in the garden and asked his permission to enter the Lisieux Carmel. She was only fourteen, and it was against the rule of the Carmelites to accept such a young candidate, but Louis arranged an appointment with the superior of the Carmelite friars. The superior believed that Thérèse was indulging in some romantic fantasy about the religious life; barely concealing his irritation, he informed her that she was not eligible for admission until she was sixteen.

But Thérèse would not give up. She begged her father to make an appointment with the bishop of Bayeux, and once again Louis could not refuse anything to his "little queen." The bishop was kind, but he also insisted that Thérèse must wait. In frustration and disappointment, Thérèse burst into tears, crying so hard that the bishop put his arms around her and tried to comfort her.

To distract his unhappy child, Louis announced that he, Thérèse, and Celine were to make a pilgrimage to Rome. The churches and shrines of Rome thrilled Thérèse and Celine, but they took-

second place to what would be the highlight of the tour—attending a Mass celebrated by Pope Leo XIII in his private chapel, followed by a private audience with the Holy Father. The pilgrims' chaplain reminded everyone that they were not to speak to the pope, simply kneel and receive his blessing. Thérèse, however, was not about to let such an opportunity pass. As she knelt before Pope Leo, she asked him to let her enter the Carmel immediately. The chaplain assured the Holy Father that the bishop of Bayeux was considering the matter. "Very well, my child," Leo said, "do as your superiors tell you."

Thérèse would not let it end there. Grabbing the pope's knees, she tried to persuade him. When Thérèse would not let go, some papal guards stepped forward, pried her hands off the pope, and carried her out of the audience chamber.

On New Year's Day, 1888, the bishop of Bayeux granted Thérèse permission to enter the Carmel early. The prioress of the Carmel, Mother Marie de Gonzague, apparently was not pleased that an exception had been made, so she put Thérèse off until after Easter.

On April 9, 1888, Thérèse and her family attended Mass at the Carmel. Afterward, she embraced her father, then walked through the door of the grill that separated the public from the nuns. There the prioress and all the nuns—including Pauline and Marie—were waiting to welcome her.

The Carmelite superior who had suspected that Thérèse had a romantic notion of convent life was correct. For all her fervor—and it was intense—Thérèse was still a fifteen-year-old girl; the daily routine of prayer, work, penances, silence, of abbreviated hours of sleep and restricted meals, clashed with her adolescent impulses and desires. She loved God profoundly, she wanted nothing so much than to devote her life to serving him, nonetheless, she had to admit that initially she found "more thorns than roses" in the Carmel. As a postulant she was assigned housekeeping chores, including washing clothes and scrubbing floors. Thérèse had never done such work in her life—her parents had servants to do all the housework. She found such work pure drudgery, and to make matters worse, Thérèse was bad at it. So in addition to the tedium, she had to endure the humiliation of being told that she had not cleaned a floor thoroughly, or had failed to get a stain out of a habit, or had not scoured all the encrusted food from a pot or pan.

Her older sisters, Pauline and Marie, still treated Thérèse as the baby of the family; even in the Carmel they wanted to pamper her. They appealed to the prioress to give Thérèse more agreeable jobs. When winter came, they returned to the prioress to ask if their little sister could be dispensed from wearing sandals and given fur-lined boots instead. Mother Marie rejected these appeals. Worse, word of them spread in the convent, so that some of the nuns began to grumble that the Martin sisters were creating a family clique in the Carmel.

Then came unhappy news from home: Louis had suffered a stroke. In the months that followed, he suffered several more. By the time he died in 1894, he was an invalid, unable to walk, barely able to speak, his mind clouded by dementia. After Louis' death, Celine joined her sisters in the Carmel.

Before dawn on Good Friday, 1896, Thérèse awoke to feel her mouth filling up with blood. It was the first sign that she had contracted tuberculosis. The Carmelite rule required a nun to inform her superior that she was ill. Thérèse told Mother Marie what had happened, but assured her that she felt perfectly well, and did not want to be dispensed from attending the Good Friday service or from keeping the Good Friday fast. Over the next year, Thérèse's condition worsened, yet she never asked Mother Marie to mitigate the severe life of the Carmel, nor did Mother Marie ever offer to do so.

By spring, 1897, however, Thérèse was too ill to follow the routine of the Carmel. She was almost completely confined to her bed now, although on warm days she would be carried to a bed in the convent garden. She was often in pain; the attending physician offered to give Thérèse injections of morphine, but Mother Marie would not permit it.

Mother Marie de Ganzague's conduct during the final months of Thérèse's life has been a source of debate. Some biographers of St. Thérèse believe

Mother Marie felt a strong animosity for Thérèse, while others argue that Mother Marie's actions were influenced by the spirit of self-sacrifice that lies at the heart of the Carmelite vocation.

In the final weeks of her life, Thérèse was in constant pain. "What is the good of writing beautifully about suffering," she said. "It means nothing, nothing!" On another occasion when she felt she was suffocating she gasped out an appeal to the Blessed Mother. "Holy Virgin," she said, "I can get no earthly air!" In her agony, Thérèse experienced a dark night of the soul, and almost despaired of God's mercy, but before the end came, she was reconciled to her sufferings.

On the evening of September 30, 1897, it was obvious that Thérèse was dying. The entire community gathered around her bed to recite the prayers for the dying. Thérèse looked at her crucifix and said, "O, I love him! My God, I love you!" A moment later she was dead. Thérèse Martin was 24 years old.

30 Days with
SAINT THÉRÈSE

❧❧❧ DAY 1 ❧❧❧❧❧❧❧❧❧❧❧❧❧❧❧❧❧❧

The Little Way

God would never inspire me with desires which cannot be realized; so, in spite of my littleness, I can hope to be a Saint. I could never grow up. I must put up with myself as I am, full of imperfections, but I will find a little way to Heaven, very short and direct, an entirely new way.

STORY OF A SOUL, CH. 9

Truly, I say to you, unless you turn and become like children, you will never enter the kingdom of heaven. Whoever humbles himself like this child, he is the greatest in the kingdom of heaven.

MATTHEW 18:3–4

Today's Meditation

St. Thérèse's "little way" is remarkably simple, yet incredibly profound: every action, every duty, no matter how insignificant can help you grow in holiness if you resolve to do it for love of God. With that thought in mind, the drudgery of housework, your most boring assignment on the job, anything at all can become a way to draw closer to Almighty God.

Prayer

Almighty God, everything I do today I will do for love of you. Give me patience and persistence to perform all of my tasks well, always with you in mind, and quell in me any spirit of rebellion or self-pity.

St. Thérèse, the Little Flower, pray for me!

✤✤✤ **DAY** 2 ✤✤✤✤✤✤✤✤✤✤✤✤✤✤✤✤✤✤✤✤✤✤✤

The Beloved's Garden

I saw that every flower He has created has a beauty of its own, that the splendor of the rose and the lily's whiteness do not deprive the violet of its scent nor make less ravishing the daisy's charm. I saw that if every little flower wished to be a rose, Nature would lose her spring adornments, and the fields would be no longer enameled with their varied flowers. So it is in the world of souls, the living garden of the Lord.

STORY OF A SOUL, CH. 1

I am a rose of Sharon, a lily of the valleys. As a lily among brambles, so is my love among maidens. As an apple tree among the trees of the wood, so is my beloved.

SONG OF SONGS 2:1–3

Today's Meditation

In the spiritual life, souls who are roses or lilies are rare. Most of us are daisies. But look on the bright side: daisies are lovely, they grow in abundance, and among garden flowers they are low-maintenance. Furthermore, better to be a daisy in Christ's garden than the most exotic lily outside it.

Prayer

Lord Jesus Christ, I praise you and give you thanks for the talents and blessings you have showered upon me. Teach me to strive to do better where I can, to accept my limitations, and to recognize that these limitations are also gifts from you. And give me the grace of humility, Lord.

St. Thérèse, the Little Flower, pray for me!

❧❧❧ DAY 3 ❧❧❧❧❧❧❧❧❧❧❧❧❧❧❧❧❧❧❧❧

God Knows Your Weakness

That I often fall asleep during meditation, or while making my thanksgiving, should appall me. Well, I am not appalled; I bear in mind that little children are just as pleasing to their parents asleep as awake.

STORY OF A SOUL, CH. 8

As a father pities his children, so the Lord pities those who fear him. For he knows our frame; he remembers that we are dust.

PSALM 103:13–14

Today's Meditation

Sometimes, are you distracted at Mass? Are there days when you rush through your prayers? By all means, strive to improve, but if these failings creep up again, don't be too hard on yourself. We all fall far short of the ideal, but that does not trouble God. As long as we try, for love of him, to perform our religious obligations faithfully, he will overlook our weaknesses.

Prayer

My God, I love you! I do not have the words to express that love. I do not have the skill to show my love. These things I accept as the result of the Fall of Adam and Eve. Yet I am truly sorry when I am at Mass or praying and my mind wanders away from you. You know that I love you. Send me your grace so I can do better.

St. Thérèse, the Little Flower, pray for me!

✣✣✣ DAY 4 ✣✣✣✣✣✣✣✣✣✣✣✣✣✣✣✣✣✣✣✣

The Power of Prayer

The power of prayer is certainly wonderful. One might liken it to a queen who always has free access to the king and can obtain everything she asks.

STORY OF A SOUL, CH. 10

When the king saw Queen Esther standing in the court, she found favor in his sight and he held out to Esther the golden scepter that was in his hand. Then Esther approached and touched the top of the scepter. And the king said to her, "What is it, Queen Esther? What is your request? It shall be given you, even to the half of my kingdom."

ESTHER 5:2–3

Today's Meditation

The souls in heaven—all the angels, all the saints—are in an enviable position. They see God face to face, and they can present your prayers and petitions to him. Ask St. Thérèse, the Blessed Mother, and your other favorite saints to pray for you, and know that God delights in their tender care for you.

Prayer

St. Thérèse, when you were a child your father called you his "little queen." Now, as a glorified saint in heaven, you are a true queen, with the privilege of asking Christ our King for graces and favors. Present my petitions to him, St. Thérèse. I have confidence in your friendship, as I have confidence in Jesus' mercy.

St. Thérèse, the Little Flower, pray for me!

✤✤✤ DAY 5 ✤✤✤✤✤✤✤✤✤✤✤✤✤✤✤✤✤✤✤✤

A Pure Soul

Jesus, my Divine Spouse, grant that I may ever keep my baptismal robe spotless. Take me from this world rather than let me tarnish my soul by one small voluntary fault. May I seek and find You alone! May no mortal creatures absorb my heart, nor I theirs! May nothing in the world ever disturb my peace!

STORY OF A SOUL, CH. 8

Clear thou me from hidden faults. Keep back thy servant also from presumptuous sins; let them not have dominion over me! Then I shall be blameless, and innocent of great transgression. Let the words of my mouth and the meditation of my heart be acceptable in thy sight, O Lord, my rock and my redeemer.

PSALM 19:12–14

Today's Meditation

We have sullied our baptismal robe with countless sins. But don't be discouraged! There is no
sin, no matter how dreadful, that God will not
forgive. But you must make an effort—repent,
go to Confession, resolve not to sin again, and
you will experience the boundless mercy of
God.

Prayer

*When I consider my sins, O God, I blush with
shame. But when I recall your loving kindness
My heart overflows with gratitude and joy.
Help me to turn away from sin, especially the
old habitual sins that are so difficult to conquer,
and prompt me to go to Confession more often
than I do now.*

St. Thérèse, the Little Flower, pray for me!

❖❖❖ DAY 6 ❖❖❖❖❖❖❖❖❖❖❖❖❖❖❖❖❖❖❖❖

Trust the Little Way

She told her novices that if she found she was wrong about her "Little Way" she would make sure they ceased to follow it. "I would come back to earth at once and tell you to go another way. If I do not come back, then believe that this is true: 'We can never have too much confidence in our God, who is so mighty and merciful.

STORY OF A SOUL, EPILOGUE

I am the way, and the truth, and the life; no one comes to the Father, but by me.

JOHN 14:6

Today's Meditation

Have no fear of following St. Thérèse's Little Way. The Church has endorsed it, particularly Blessed Pope John Paul II. In 1997, when he proclaimed St. Thérèse of Lisieux a Doctor of the Church, he said that in her Little Way "we can discern an enlightened witness of faith which, while accepting with trusting love God's merciful condescension and salvation in Christ, reveals the mystery and holiness of the Church."

Prayer

St. Thérèse, as I begin to follow your Little Way, pray for me that I will be faithful so that everyday I may grow a little more holy, a little more patient with tiresome people, and a little more obedient to the will of God.

St. Thérèse, the Little Flower, pray for me!

❖❖❖ **DAY** 7 ❖❖❖❖❖❖❖❖❖❖❖❖❖❖❖❖❖

The Love of Sinners

I have often heard it said in retreats and elsewhere that an innocent soul never loves God as much as a repentant one, and how I long to prove that that is not true.

STORY OF A SOUL, CH. 4

Behold, a woman of the city, who was a sinner, when she learned that [Jesus] was at table in the Pharisee's house, brought an alabaster flask of ointment, and standing behind him at his feet, weeping, she began to wet his feet with her tears, and wiped them with the hair of her head, and kissed his feet, and anointed them with the ointment.

LUKE 7:37–38

Today's Meditation

Think of the last time you had to confess a sin that especially embarrassed you. Recall the apprehension you felt before you confessed it. Now remember the sense of relief you felt after you received absolution. And not just relief, but profound gratitude to Almighty God, who gave us this sacrament so we can be restored to him.

Prayer

I am a sinner, Lord. Yet I love you for all the graces you give to me, every moment of every day. Most particularly I thank you for granting to your priests the power to absolve sins. At that moment, I understand how the Prodigal Son must have felt when his father welcomed him back to his family. Like the Prodigal Son I have nothing of value to give you, Lord. Accept, then, my gratitude and my love.

St. Thérèse, the Little Flower, pray for me!

✤✤✤ DAY 8 ✤✤✤✤✤✤✤✤✤✤✤✤✤✤✤✤✤✤✤

Cultivate Your Soul

How many souls might reach a high degree of
sanctity if properly directed from the first. I know
God can sanctify souls without help, but just as He
gives the gardener the skill to tend rare and delicate
plants while fertilizing them Himself, so He wishes
to use others in His cultivation of souls.

STORY OF A SOUL, CH. 5

*Even the sparrow finds a home, and the swallow
a nest for herself, where she may lay her young, at
thy altars, O Lord of hosts, my King and my God.
Blessed are those who dwell in thy house, ever singing thy praise!*

PSALM 84:3–4

Today's Meditation

Have you noticed that most priests have spiritual directors, yet very few laypeople do? It is their seminary training that revealed to our priests that if they want to grow closer to Christ, they need the help of a fellow priest who is experienced in the spiritual life. If you are serious about cultivating your soul, find a spiritual director to show you the way.

Prayer

By fits and starts I have tried to draw closer to you, good Lord. And you see how poor has been my progress. Send me an experienced spiritual director to be my guide so that I can see the wisdom of turning away from everything that is shallow and corrupt and embrace what is eternal, perfect, and true—that is, yourself.

St. Thérèse, the Little Flower, pray for me!

✿✿✿ DAY 9 ✿✿✿✿✿✿✿✿✿✿✿✿✿✿✿✿✿✿✿✿

Humbly Submit to Christ

To remain little—it is to recognize our nothingness, to expect everything from the good God, not to be too much afflicted about our faults . . . in fine, it is *not* to make one's fortune, nor to be disquieted about anything.

COUNSELS AND REMINISCENCES
THOUGHTS OF ST. THÉRÈSE, P. 113

Bud like a rose growing by a stream of water; send forth fragrance like frankincense, and put forth blossoms like a lily. Scatter the fragrance, and sing a hymn of praise; bless the Lord for all his works; ascribe majesty to his name and give thanks to him with praise, with songs on your lips.

SIRACH 39:13–15

Today's Meditation

Humility and simplicity of heart are the hall-marks of St. Thérèse's Little Way. It calls upon you to stop obsessing about your sins, to trust in the goodness of God, to recognize that true contrition coupled with love for God and neighbor can make your soul bud like a rose.

Prayer

Intercede for me, St. Thérèse, so that I can be more like you: content to be modest, not looking for praise and attention, delighting in offering to God the countless little things that make up my day.

St. Thérèse, the Little Flower, pray for me!

❖❖❖ DAY 10 ❖❖❖❖❖❖❖❖❖❖❖❖❖❖❖❖❖

A Spiritual Bouquet

One Sunday, for example, I went to see [Mother Genevieve of St. Teresa, the foundress of the Lisieux Carmel] in the infirmary and found two of the older Sisters with her. I was discreetly beating a retreat when she called me back, saying, as if in some way inspired: "Wait, my child, I have something to say to you. You are always asking for a spiritual bouquet; very well, today I give you this one: 'Serve God in peace and joy, and remember, our God is the God of Peace.'"

STORY OF A SOUL, CH. 8

Grace is poured upon your lips; therefore God has blessed you for ever.

PSALM 45:2

Today's Meditation

There is no telling where inspiration will come from. You may expect to find it in the Bible, or the writings of the saints and mystics—and you *will* find it there. But many times it will come from a friend or acquaintance, who, unbeknownst to himself, has brought you a message from God.

Prayer

Open my heart and my ears, O Lord, so that I will always be ready to hear your voice. Let me follow it along the narrow path that leads to eternal life. Let nothing distract me from the great goal of my life—at last seeing you face to face.

St. Thérèse, the Little Flower, pray for me!

✥✥✥ DAY 11 ✥✥✥✥✥✥✥✥✥✥✥✥✥✥✥✥✥

A Tabernacle for Jesus

I think of my soul as a piece of waste ground and ask Our Lady to take away the rubbish of my imperfections and then build a spacious tabernacle there, worthy of Heaven, adorning it with her own loveliness. Then I invite the Angels and the Saints to come and sing canticles of love; it seems to me that Jesus is glad to be magnificently received like this, and I share His joy.

STORY OF A SOUL, CH. 8

Who shall ascend the hill of the Lord? And who shall stand in his holy place? He who has clean hands and a pure heart, who does not lift up his soul to what is false, and does not swear deceitfully. He will receive blessing from the Lord, and vindication from the God of his salvation.

PSALM 24:3–5

Today's Meditation

Every time you receive Holy Communion worthily, you become a living tabernacle for Jesus. Pray and make sacrifices so that you will always be prepared to welcome Our Lord in the Blessed Sacrament into your heart.

Prayer

St. Thérèse, pray for me so that I may never receive Holy Communion while in state a of serious sin. Then inspire me to do all that I can to make my heart and soul a worthy place to receive Christ our God.

St. Thérèse, the Little Flower, pray for me!

❖❖❖ **DAY** 12 ❖❖❖❖❖❖❖❖❖❖❖❖❖❖❖❖

The Mission of the Angels

Angels do not remain here below once their task is done. They wing their way back to God. That is why they have wings.

STORY OF A SOUL, CH. 8

Behold, I send an angel before you, to guard you on the way and to bring you to the place, which I have prepared. Give heed to him and hearken to his voice, do not rebel against him.

EXODUS 23:20–21

TODAY'S MEDITATION

In heaven the angels praise God without ceasing, and on earth they protect God's people constantly. The Bible and the history of the Church tells of the many times when angels have intervened on our behalf—sometimes in very dramatic ways.

PRAYER

All you holy angels, my Guardian Angel in particular, I thank you for the many times you have inspired me to do good, have kept me safe from harm, and prompted me to be a loving child of God. Stir up our Holy Father the Pope, our bishops, priests and religious, and all people of good will to desire to do the will of God without counting the cost.

St. Thérèse, the Little Flower, pray for me!

❦❦❦ DAY 13 ❦❦❦❦❦❦❦❦❦❦❦❦❦❦❦❦❦❦

The Way of Love

How sweet the way of Love, Mother! One can fall, I know; there may be infidelities, yet Love knows how *to turn all things to profit*, quickly consuming everything which might displease Jesus, and leaving at the bottom of one's heart nothing but deep and humble peace.

STORY OF A SOUL, CH. 8

O taste and see that the Lord is good! Happy is the man who takes refuge in him! O fear the Lord, you his saints, for those who fear him have no want!

PSALM 34:8–9

Today's Meditation

In heaven as on earth, there is nothing that love cannot cure. If you love God, you will never fall too far away from him. If you love God, no matter how serious your sins, you will always repent and return to him. Remember, even the saints were not perfectly faithful to God, and he does not expect perfection from us. As long as you love him, he will return that love a thousand-fold.

Prayer

O God, I am weak and at times I fail in my fidelity to you. Yet it is my heartfelt prayer that you will increase my love for you so that at the end of my life I will not be separated for all eternity from your love. Fill my heart with love for you, and each day draw me a little closer to you.

St. Thérèse, the Little Flower, pray for me!

❧❧❧ DAY 14 ❧❧❧❧❧❧❧❧❧❧❧❧❧❧❧❧❧

The Kingdom of God Is Within You

During meditation I am sustained above all else by the Gospels. They supply my poor soul's every need, and they are always yielding up to me new lights and mysterious hidden meanings. I know from experience that *"the Kingdom of God is within us."*

STORY OF A SOUL, CH. 8

The kingdom of God is not coming with signs to be observed; nor will they say, "Lo, here it is!" or "There!" for behold, the kingdom of God is in the midst of you.

LUKE 17:20–21

Today's Meditation

Heaven is the perfect kingdom of God. But when Our Lord was personally present here on earth, he taught us to establish a new society that would reflect the perfection of heaven. Whenever you act with charity, patience, forbearance, and mercy, you build up the kingdom of God here on earth.

Prayer

Give me your grace, good Lord, to be selfless and courageous in building the kingdom of God among men. Help me to imitate St. Thérèse, who came to understand how much you love us when we perform little acts of kindness for our neighbor. Let me never put off doing good, no matter how small that act may seem.

St. Thérèse, the Little Flower, pray for me!

❧❧❧ DAY 15 ❧❧❧❧❧❧❧❧❧❧❧❧❧❧❧❧

Harken to the Voice of God

Jesus has no need of books or doctors to instruct our soul; He, the Doctor of Doctors, teaches us without the sound of words. I have never heard Him speak, and yet I know He is within my soul. Every moment He is guiding and inspiring me, and just at the moment I need them, "lights" till then unseen are granted me.

STORY OF A SOUL, CH. 8

And the Lord came and stood forth, calling as at other times, "Samuel! Samuel!" And Samuel said, "Speak, for thy servant hears." Then the Lord said to Samuel, "Behold, I am about to do a thing."

1 SAMUEL 3:10

Today's Meditation

Every day, all day long, God calls to you, inviting you to do his will. In the noise and busyness of daily life, it is easy to ignore God's call, to pretend that you do not hear him. Be attentive, and see what marvelous things God will do once you submit to him.

Prayer

Speak, Lord, for your servant is listening. Give me strength to do your will. Reveal to me the joy that comes from serving you. Enlighten my mind so I may see that what the world offers me are empty distractions, and that my heart will be restless until it rests in you.

St. Thérèse, the Little Flower, pray for me!

Different Gifts

But then I realized that we cannot all be alike; there must be different kinds of holiness to glorify the divine perfections.

STORY OF A SOUL, CH. 8

His gifts were that some should be apostles, some prophets, some evangelists, some pastors and teachers, to equip the saints for the work of ministry, for building up the body of Christ.

EPHESIANS 4:11–12

Today's Meditation

No matter what your state of life may be, you have gifts that can be of use to the Church and your neighbor. Make an honest assessment of your God-given talents and consider if you are doing all that you can to build up the body of Christ.

Prayer

Teach me to be grateful, Lord, for the gifts you have given me, and not to resent or mourn the gifts you gave to others. Help me to see what I can do to help my neighbors, my parish, and the Church at large, and give me the resolve to do those things as well as I am able.

St. Thérèse, the Little Flower, pray for me!

Christ Loves the Weak

To me He has manifested His Infinite Mercy, and it is in this shining mirror that I gaze upon His other attributes, which there appear all radiant with love—all, even justice. What joy to remember that Our Lord is just, that He makes allowances for all our shortcomings and knows full well how weak we are. What have I to fear then?

STORY OF A SOUL, CH. 8

Steadfast love and faithfulness will meet; righteousness and peace will kiss each other. Faithfulness will spring up from the ground, and righteousness will look down from the sky. Yea, the Lord will give what is good, and our land will yield its increase.

PSALM 85:10–12

Today's Meditation

St. Thérèse is correct: Christ's justice is tempered by his mercy and his love for us. But do not assume that you can live a godless life and gain eternal salvation in the end. You must strive to be holy, you must repent for all your sins and failings, and try, with God's grace, to do better. Only then will you experience the mercy of Jesus.

Prayer

Lord Jesus Christ, never let me be parted from you. Turn away all the temptations and distractions of this world that serve no other purpose than to keep me from union with you. Give me the grace of perfect confidence in you, and the grace to be worthy of your mercy.

St. Thérèse, the Little Flower, pray for me!

❖❖❖ DAY 18 ❖❖❖❖❖❖❖❖❖❖❖❖❖❖❖❖❖❖❖❖

You Shall Be Lifted Up

We live in the age of inventions now, and the wealthy no longer have to take the trouble to climb the stairs; they take an elevator. That is what I must find, *an elevator* to take me straight up to Jesus, because I am too little to climb the steep stairway of perfection.

STORY OF A SOUL, CH. 9

And a highway shall be there, and it shall be called the Holy Way; the unclean shall not pass over it, and fools shall not err therein. No lion shall be there, nor shall any ravenous beast come up on it; they shall not be found there, but the redeemed shall walk there. And the ransomed of the Lord shall return, and come to Zion with singing.

ISAIAH 35:8–10

Today's Meditation

The message of the gospel does not try to trick you or trip you up. It is not onerous. It is not a burden. By dying on the Cross and rising from the dead, Christ made the way to heaven easy: faith in him, worthy reception of the sacraments, prayer—particularly the Holy Sacrifice of the Mass—and acts of charity.

Prayer

I live in dark and confusing times, O Lord. Yet I long for you with all my heart. Shine your light so I can see the way that leads to you. Raise me up when I am discouraged, and at the end of my time here on earth, lift me to the glory of your kingdom.

St. Thérèse, the Little Flower, pray for me!

DAY 19

Take Up Your Cross

Yet I realize as never before that the Lord is gentle and merciful; He did not send me this heavy cross until I could bear it. If He had sent it before, I am certain that it would have discouraged me, but now it merely takes away from me any natural satisfaction I might feel in longing for Heaven.

STORY OF A SOUL, CH. 9

If any man would come after me, let him deny himself and take up his cross daily and follow me. For whoever would save his life will lose it; and whoever loses his life for my sake, he will save it.

LUKE 9:23–24

Today's Meditation

Look at the crucifix: God the Father did not spare His only Son from suffering, pain, and death. How then can any of us complain of the troubles that come our way? When sorrows come, ask God to give you the strength to bear them. Unite your suffering with the Passion of Jesus Christ, and ask for the consolation of the Blessed Virgin Mary, Our Lady of Sorrows.

Prayer

Holy Mary, Mother of God, I cannot imagine the anguish you experienced as you stood at the foot of the Cross and watched your Son die. Come and share my troubles and support me, as St. John and St. Mary Magdalene supported you. Give me courage to accept my cross, and the strength to bear it. And never let me forget that the way of the Cross ends with resurrection.

St. Thérèse, the Little Flower, pray for me!

❧❧❧ **DAY 20** ❧❧❧❧❧❧❧❧❧❧❧❧❧❧❧❧❧❧❧

The Beauty of Ordinary Things

"In my 'little way,' everything is most ordinary;
everything I do must be within the reach of other
little souls also."

STORY OF A SOUL, EPILOGUE

*And he sat down opposite the treasury, and watched
the multitude putting money into the treasury. Many
rich people put in large sums. And a poor widow
came, and put in two copper coins, which make a
penny. And he called his disciples to him, and said to
them, "Truly, I say to you, this poor widow has put
in more than all those who are contributing to the
treasury. For they all contributed out of their abundance; but she out of her poverty has put in everything she had, her whole living."*

MARK 12:41–44

Today's Meditation

It is unlikely that you are a mystic who receives heavenly visions, or a miracle worker with a healing touch, or a profound theologian who explores the mysteries of God, or a future martyr with undaunted courage. In other words, you are most likely like almost everyone else: one of the ordinary children of God. That is why St. Thérèse's little way is ideal for you.

Prayer

Almighty God, the men, women, and children the Church honors as saints and blesseds served you heroically. I fall short of their high standard, O Lord, yet I want to love and serve you. Accept my humble efforts as you accepted the widow's mite. And never let me be ambitious for anything but the joy of eternal life with you.

St. Thérèse, the Little Flower, pray for me!

Food Ever New

I have often noticed that Jesus will not give me a store of provisions; He nourishes me with food that is entirely new from moment to moment, and I find it in my soul without knowing how it got there. In all simplicity, I believe that Jesus Himself is, in a mysterious way, at work in the depths of my soul, inspiring me with whatever He wants me to do at that moment.

STORY OF A SOUL, CH. 8

The thoughts of his heart are to all generations. . . .
Behold, the eye of the Lord is on those who fear him,
on those who hope in his steadfast love, that he may
deliver their soul from death, and keep them alive in
famine.

PSALM 33:11, 18–19

TODAY'S MEDITATION

The human body is a complex machine, and out of his love and mercy, God sustains yours moment by moment. But he is not just a Divine Technician, he is our Savior, and so he grants to you inspirations and consolations—if you are alert to them. And the best way to remain alert is to remain in a state of grace.

PRAYER

Your Sacred Heart, Good Jesus, is on fire with love for all mankind. Touch my heart so that it is never indifferent to you or cold to the neighbor who needs me. Make it sensitive to the consolations you sent to St. Thérèse, and let it always be a worthy dwelling place for you.

St. Thérèse, the Little Flower, pray for me!

✤✤✤ DAY 22 ✤✤✤✤✤✤✤✤✤✤✤✤✤✤✤✤

The Victim of Love

Can a victim of love find anything her Spouse sends terrible? Every moment He sends what I can bear and no more; He increases my strength to meet my pain.

STORY OF A SOUL, EPILOGUE

You have ravished my heart, my sister, my bride, you have ravished my heart. . . . A garden locked is my sister, my bride, a garden locked, a fountain sealed.

SONG OF SONGS 4:9, 12

Today's Meditation

Trials, unhappiness, disappointments, illness—sufferings of all kinds are part of our life on earth. Yet some people seem to be more afflicted than others. St. Thérèse was only twenty-four when she died, in great pain, from tuberculosis. Yet even on her deathbed she assured her sisters that God gave her the strength to bear her suffering.

Prayer

Give me the strength to bear what I must bear, good Lord. Increase my confidence that you will never desert me. And if there is anything I can do to alleviate my distress, clear my mind so that I can see it and act swiftly. In this, as in all things, Jesus, I trust in you.

St. Thérèse, the Little Flower, pray for me!

❀❀❀ DAY 23 ❀❀❀❀❀❀❀❀❀❀❀❀❀❀❀❀❀❀❀

The Master's Will

All these friends of God have followed the guidance of the Holy Spirit, who inspired the Prophet to write: *"Tell the just man that all is well."* (Cf. Is. 3:10). Yes, all is well when one seeks nothing but the Divine Will.

STORY OF A SOUL, CH. 9

But seek first his kingdom and his righteousness, and all these things shall be yours as well.

MATTHEW 6:33

Today's Meditation

We are willful, stubborn creatures. And at times it can be difficult to submit to the will of God, particularly if he has taken to himself a loved one, or sent us a deep disappointment, or demanded that we give up a secret vice. Yet all the saints knew that resistance only makes us more miserable.

Prayer

Give me your grace, Lord, to accept your holy will. Put an end to my rebellious spirit. Console me in my time of trouble. All my hope is in you.

St. Thérèse, the Little Flower, pray for me!

✠✠✠ DAY 24 ✠✠✠✠✠✠✠✠✠✠✠✠✠✠✠✠✠✠✠

Unhappy Souls

Jesus taught me that there really are souls who by
their abuse of grace have lost the precious treasures
of faith and hope, and with them all joy that is pure
and true.

STORY OF A SOUL, CH. 9

*So faith, hope, love abide, these three; but the great-
est of these is love.*

1 CORINTHIANS 13:13

Today's Meditation

It is tragic that so many of our friends and neighbors live without faith, and some even without hope. What a bleak world they inhabit. Yet even we who consider ourselves faithful to God have times of confusion and doubt. Even St. Thérèse, as she was dying, wondered if perhaps God had abandoned her. But he had not. He never abandons us—that is the foundation of our faith and the cause of our hope.

Prayer

I give you thanks, Almighty God, for having given to me the great gift of faith. Increase in me daily the virtues of faith, hope, and charity. And grant me your grace so that I may not only profess these virtues, but live them everyday.

St. Thérèse, the Little Flower, pray for me!

❖❖❖ DAY 25 ❖❖❖❖❖❖❖❖❖❖❖❖❖❖❖❖❖❖❖❖

Love Is Patient

I see now that true charity consists in bearing with
the faults of those about us, never being surprised
at their weaknesses, but edified at the least sign of
virtue.

STORY OF A SOUL, CH. 9

Love is patient and kind; love is not jealous or boast-
ful; it is not arrogant or rude. Love does not insist
on its own way; it is not irritable or resentful; it does
not rejoice at wrong, but rejoices in the right. Love
bears all things, believes all things, hopes all things,
endures all things.

1 CORINTHIANS 13:4–7

Today's Meditation

St. John Bosco once said that one of the greatest penances we can impose upon ourselves is to be patient and cheerful with irritating people. It was part of St. Thérèse's Little Way to find something to admire even in people she disliked—she found it reduced her antipathy for those people and made her less ill at ease around them.

Prayer

Forgive me, dear Jesus, when I have failed to see you in my neighbors. Give me your grace so I may recognize you in all your children. Teach me patience and compassion. And let me learn to forgive those who do not like me.

St. Thérèse, the Little Flower, pray for me!

❖❖❖ DAY 26 ❖❖❖❖❖❖❖❖❖❖❖❖❖❖❖❖❖

Pray As a Child

I have not the courage to make myself search for wonderful prayers in books; there are so many of them, and it gives me a headache. In any case, each one seems more beautiful than the one before. As I cannot say all of them, and do not know which to choose, I just act like a child who can't read; I tell God, quite simply, all that I want to say, and He always understands.

STORY OF A SOUL, CH. 10

Ask, and it will be given you; seek, and you will find; knock, and it will be opened to you. For every one who asks receives, and he who seeks finds, and to him who knocks it will be opened.

MATTHEW 7:7–8

Today's Meditation

Pray to God for all the graces necessary for your soul's salvation—he will not refuse you. That is what Jesus promises in today's text from St. Matthew's gospel. We are quick to pray for our temporal needs, but don't neglect to pray for your spiritual needs, too.

Prayer

O God, let me not be so caught up in the busyness of this world that I forget to prepare for the next. I beg you, grant me all the virtues and graces necessary to serve you here are earth so that at the end of my life I may join you forever in your kingdom.

St. Thérèse, the Little Flower, pray for me!

✣✣✣ DAY 27 ✣✣✣✣✣✣✣✣✣✣✣✣✣✣✣✣✣✣

The Wisdom of Solomon

I have every reason, Mother, to be most grateful to God, and I am going to let you into another precious secret. He has shown the same mercy to me as He did to King Solomon. He has granted me every wish.

STORY OF A SOUL, CH. 8

I give you also what you have not asked, both riches and honor, so that no other king shall compare with you, all your days. And if you will walk in my ways, keeping my statutes and my commandments, as your father David walked, then I will lengthen your days.

1 KINGS 3:13–14

Today's Meditation

When Solomon became king of Israel, God asked him what he desired most. Solomon asked for wisdom. God gave Solomon wisdom, and gave him many temporal gifts as well. Consider how abundantly God has blessed you, and continues to bless you, and do not be afraid to ask him to continue his goodness to you.

Prayer

My Lord and my God! You are my benefactor, my defender, my consolation, my savior. Come and dwell in my heart, let me have you always foremost in my mind so that all my thoughts and actions may be pleasing to you.

St. Thérèse, the Little Flower, pray for me!

❧❧❧ DAY 28 ❧❧❧❧❧❧❧❧❧❧❧❧❧❧❧❧❧❧

The Gift of Peace

O Jesus, it is peace I beg of You. Peace, and above all, boundless love. . . . I offer myself to You, my Beloved, that You may do in me everything You will, unhindered by any created obstacle.

STORY OF A SOUL, CH. 8

The Lord bless you and keep you:
The Lord make his face to shine upon you, and be
  gracious to you:
The Lord lift up his countenance upon you, and
  give you peace.

NUMBERS 6:24–26

Today's Meditation

When Christians pray for peace, we pray for the end of all wars, but also for the elimination of anger, hatred, and the desire for revenge from human hearts. We also pray for peace on a deeper level—the peace of soul and mind that comes from faith in the goodness of Almighty God.

Prayer

O God, from whom proceeds all holy desires, right counsels, and just works, give to your servants that peace which the world cannot give; that our hearts may be disposed to obey your commandments, and the fear of enemies being removed, our times, by your protection, may be peaceful. Through Christ our Lord, Amen.

St. Thérèse, the Little Flower, pray for me!

✿✿✿ DAY 29 ✿✿✿✿✿✿✿✿✿✿✿✿✿✿✿✿✿✿✿✿✿

A Very Little Soul

So you see, Mother, what a very *little soul* I am! I can only offer very *little things* to God. These little sacrifices bring great peace of soul, but I often let the chance of making them slip by. However, it does not discourage me. I put up with having a little less peace, and try to be more careful the next time.

STORY OF A SOUL, CH. 10

For truly, I say to you, if you have faith as a grain of mustard seed, you will say to this mountain, 'Move from here to there,' and it will move; and nothing will be impossible to you.

MATTHEW 17:7

TODAY'S MEDITATION

God is pleased by even the smallest sacrifice you make in his name. As you make sacrifice after sacrifice, imperceptibly you will be growing in holiness. And the holier you become, the less this world, with all its troubles, has a hold on you.

PRAYER

Good Jesus, today and every day for the rest of my life I will perform all my tasks and obligations for love of you. I will make at least one sacrifice for your sake. Be pleased to accept such humble offerings, dear Lord, and give me your grace so that each day I will draw a little closer to you.

St. Thérèse, the Little Flower, pray for me!

✤✤✤ **DAY** 30 ✤✤✤✤✤✤✤✤✤✤✤✤✤✤✤✤✤

Love God with All Your Heart

I have given nothing but love to God and He will repay with love. After my death I will let fall a shower of roses.

STORY OF A SOUL, EPILOGUE

My beloved speaks and says to me: "Arise, my love, my fair one, and come away; for lo, the winter is past, the rain is over and gone. The flowers appear on the earth, the time of singing has come."

SONGS OF SONGS 2:10–12

Today's Meditation

It was love for God that moved St. Thérèse to follow her little way. And as she practiced it, her love for God increased, and she found that she was more conscious of God's immense love for her.

Prayer

O Little Flower of Jesus, in your unfailing intercession I place my trust. Petition Our Blessed Savior to grant the blessing of which I stand in greatest need [mention your petition here]. Shower upon me your promised roses of virtue and grace, dear Saint Thérèse, so that swiftly advancing in sanctity and in perfect love of neighbor, I may someday receive the crown of eternal life. Amen.

St. Thérèse, the Little Flower, pray for me!

About the Author

For the last 30 years, Thomas Craughwell has been an independent scholar of the saints, digging through the autobiographies and letters of the saints, as well the writings of their contemporaries, to get past the sentimentality that tends to surround saints and find the living, breathing, struggling, real-life men and women.

Craughwell is a full-time freelance writer. Among his published works are the highly acclaimed *Saints Behaving Badly* (Doubleday, 2006), *Saints for Every Occasion* (Stampley, 2001), and *Saints Preserved: An Encyclopedia of Relics* (Image, 2011). He has written more than two dozen books on history, religion, and popular culture.

Craughwell has written about saints for *Wall Street Journal*, *American Spectator*, *Inside the Vatican*, *National Catholic Register*, and many Catholic publications. He is a regular contributor to *Our Sunday Visitor*, and writes a monthly column on patron saints for diocesan newspapers.

A popular speaker, Craughwell has appeared on EWTN, CNN, Discovery Channel and more than 150 radio stations to discuss saints, the canonization process, and Catholic history. He was also featured in The History Channel adaptation of one of his highly praised historical books, *Stealing Lincoln's Body*.

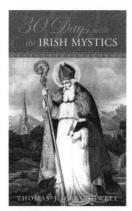